WORLD LINK 1

DEVELOPING ENGLISH FLUENCY

FOURTH EDITION
WORKBOOK

WORLD LINK 1
DEVELOPING ENGLISH FLUENCY

Australia • Brazil • Canada • Mexico • Singapore • United Kingdom • United States

National Geographic Learning,
a Cengage Company

World Link Level 1 Workbook
Fourth Edition

Publisher: Sherrise Roehr

Executive Editor: Sarah Kenney

Senior Development Editor: Lewis Thompson

Development Editor: Adam Robinson

Director of Global Marketing: Ian Martin

Heads of Regional Marketing:
  Charlotte Ellis (Europe, Middle East and Africa)
  Irina Pereyra (Latin America)

Senior Product Marketing Manager:
  Caitlin Thomas

Content Project Manager: Beth Houston

Media Researcher: Stephanie Eenigenburg

Cover/Text Design: Lisa Trager

Art Director: Brenda Carmichael

Operations Support: Hayley Chwazik-Gee, Avi Mednick

Manufacturing Planner: Mary Beth Hennebury

Composition: MPS North America LLC

© 2021 Cengage Learning, Inc.

ALL RIGHTS RESERVED. No part of this work covered by the copyright herein may be reproduced or distributed in any form or by any means, except as permitted by U.S. copyright law, without the prior written permission of the copyright owner.

"National Geographic", "National Geographic Society" and the Yellow Border Design are registered trademarks of the National Geographic Society ® Marcas Registradas

For permission to use material from this text or product, submit all requests online at **cengage.com/permissions**
Further permissions questions can be emailed to
permissionrequest@cengage.com

ISBN: 978-0-357-50376-8

National Geographic Learning
200 Pier 4 Boulevard
Boston, MA 02210
USA

Locate your local office at **international.cengage.com/region**

Visit National Geographic Learning online at **ELTNGL.com**
Visit our corporate website at **www.cengage.com**

Printed in the United States of America
Print Number: 01 Print Year: 2021

TABLE OF CONTENTS

UNIT 1 People .... **page 2**

UNIT 2 Behavior .... **page 8**

UNIT 3 Shopping .... **page 14**

UNIT 4 Vacation .... **page 20**

UNIT 5 Heroes .... **page 26**

UNIT 6 The Mind .... **page 32**

UNIT 7 City Life .... **page 38**

UNIT 8 All About You .... **page 44**

UNIT 9 Change .... **page 50**

UNIT 10 Health .... **page 56**

UNIT 11 Achievement .... **page 62**

UNIT 12 At the Movies .... **page 68**

PHOTO CREDITS

Illustrations: All illustrations are owned by © Cengage.

5 Digital Vision/Alamy Stock Photo; **12** Luca Elvira/Shutterstock.com; **20** (cl1) Brian A Jackson/Shutterstock.com, (cl2) Dudarev Mikhail/Shutterstock.com, (c1) PhotoDisc/Getty Images, (c2) iStock.com/BasSlabbers, (cr1) Corbis/Jupiterimages, (cr2) Panfilova Yanika/Alamy Stock Photo; **24** Francesco R. Iacomino/Shutterstock.com; **28** Lenscap Photography/Shutterstock.com; **30** Heidi Besen/Shutterstock.com; **31** Alejandra Matiz/Leo Matiz Foundation Mexico/Getty Images; **42** (tr) Ugurhan Betin/iStock/Getty Images, (cl) Kwest/Shutterstock.com; **54** EQRoy/Shutterstock.com; **56** Westend61/Getty Images; **61** Franny-anne/iStock/Getty Images Plus/Getty Images; **64** Kzenon/Shutterstock.com; **66** Shandor/Shutterstock.com.

PEOPLE

A GETTING TO KNOW YOU

VOCABULARY

A Complete the form with your own information.

My Profile

First name _____

Last name _____

Hometown _____

Phone number _____

Email address _____

Languages _____

Interests _____

_____

_____

B Match the questions with the answers.

1. What's your name?
2. Do you speak English?
3. Where are you from?
4. Where do you live now?
5. What's your email address?
6. How old are you?
7. What do you do?
8. What do you do for fun?

a. I'm from Japan.
b. I'm a student.
c. keiko333@memail.com.
d. Keiko Goto.
e. I'm 20.
f. Yes, I do.
g. I like to travel.
h. I live in Los Angeles.

2 | UNIT 1

CONVERSATION

A Unscramble the words to make sentences.

1. name / Tara. / is / my

   _____

2. do / you / what / do?

   _____

3. it's nice / hi, / to / you. / meet / I'm Pedro.

   _____

4. student. / I'm / English / an

   _____

5. it's / too. / you, / meet / nice / to

   _____

B Number the sentences in order to make a conversation.

   ____ a. Yes. I study art at Hunter College. What do you do, Anna?

   _1_ b. Hi. My name is Muhammad. I'm in apartment B-10.

   ____ c. Nice to meet you, too.

   ____ d. So, are you a student, Muhammad?

   ____ e. That's great.

   ____ f. I'm a student at NYU. I also work at a restaurant.

   ____ g. Hi, Muhammad. I'm Anna. I'm in C-6. It's nice to meet you.

C Now write new conversations. Use the example in **B** to help you.

1. Conversation with a classmate

   You: _____

   Classmate: _____

   You: _____

   Classmate: _____

   You: _____

   Classmate: _____

   You: _____

   Classmate: _____

2. Conversation with a teacher

   You: _____

   Teacher: _____

   You: _____

   Teacher: _____

   You: _____

   Teacher: _____

   You: _____

   Teacher: _____

GRAMMAR

A Do you do the activities in the chart? Put a (✓) for *yes* or a (✗) for *no*. Then write sentences.

✓ = Yes ✗ = no	Stephano	Cristina	Jun and Li	You
study English	✓	✗	✓	
watch movies online	✗	✓	✓	
listen to rock music	✓	✓	✗	
have a job	✗	✓	✓	

1. **Stephano** *studies English.*
   He *doesn't watch movies online.*
   He *listens to rock music.*
   He *doesn't have a job.*

2. **Cristina** _____

3. **Jun and Li** _____

4. **You** _____

B Match the questions with the answers.

1. Do they have a child?
2. Is Ms. Baker your teacher?
3. Are you from Mexico?
4. Are the new students from China?
5. Do you speak Spanish?
6. Does your mother have a job?

a. No, she isn't.
b. Yes, I do.
c. Yes, they do.
d. Yes, she does.
e. No, I'm not.
f. No, they aren't.

C Unscramble the words to make questions. Then write answers with your own information.

1. you / do / what / do _____

2. live / a / you / in / city / do _____

3. weekends / you / what / do / do / on _____

4. English / are / you / an / student _____

4 | UNIT 1

B APPEARANCE

VOCABULARY AND GRAMMAR

A Write the words in the correct columns. Then choose the words that describe you.

average (x2)	blue	gray	in your teens	old	slim	young
black	brown (x2)	green	in your twenties	red	straight	
blond	curly	heavy	long	short (x2)	tall	

Age	Height	Weight	Hair Color	Hairstyle	Eye Color

B Write sentences about yourself.

1. *My hair is* _____.
2. _____
3. _____

C Look at the photo of the family. Write one sentence about each person.

Mother: _____

Father: _____

Grandmother: _____

Grandfather: _____

Baby: _____

READING AND WRITING

A Read the emails.

1.
Date: April 16   Subject: Mr. Ryder's visit

Dear Mr. Tanaka,
Please meet Mr. James Ryder at the airport at 11:00 tomorrow. His flight is UA238 from Los Angeles. He is a tall man in his sixties with gray hair, and he wears big glasses. His meeting with the marketing department is at 4:00.
Thank you.

Kyra Greene
Marketing Department

2.
Date: April 16   Subject: Plans for tomorrow

Hi Gita,
Thanks so much for meeting my brother at the airport tomorrow. Please tell him I finish work at 3:00. His name is David, he's 32, and he looks a lot like me (short, heavy, curly, brown hair, no beard). He's coming at 11:00 on flight AA397 from Toronto.
Let's have dinner tomorrow night!
See you!

Andres

3.
Date: April 16   Subject: Car problems again!

Sun,
HELP! Can you meet my friend Tom at the airport tomorrow? My car has big problems and I can't drive it. Tom is coming on flight KX661 from Denver at 11:00. He's average height and kind of thin, with long, blond hair. Thanks a million!

Chris

B Read the emails in **A** again. For each email, write the words that describe appearance.

Email 1	Email 2	Email 3
tall man in his sixties		

6 | UNIT 1

C Look at the picture. Label each person with the correct number, based on the email descriptions in **A**. There are three extra circles.

D Read and complete the descriptions with *has*, *have*, *is*, *are*, *wear*, or *wears*.

My favorite actress is Mariana Ortiz. She **(1.)** _____ short, black hair. She **(2.)** _____ average height. She **(3.)** _____ big blue eyes and she doesn't **(4.)** _____ glasses. She **(5.)** _____ very young. I think she **(6.)** _____ in her twenties.

My favorite singers are the Bell Tones. They **(7.)** _____ in their thirties. They **(8.)** _____ all tall and thin. They **(9.)** _____ long, blond hair. The lead singer **(10.)** _____ big glasses.

E Write a description of a famous person.

_____
_____
_____
_____
_____
_____
_____

Appearance | 7

2
BEHAVIOR

A WHAT ARE YOU DOING?

VOCABULARY

A Unscramble the letters to write verbs.

1. strat _____
2. ghlau _____
3. stuoh _____
4. elims _____
5. okol _____

6. psto _____
7. chtwa _____
8. vewa _____
9. ewra _____
10. nur _____

B Choose the correct word to complete each sentence.

1. She is **starting** / **watching** TV.
2. He is **stopping** / **waving** to take a break.
3. She is **starting** / **smiling** in the photo.
4. They are not happy. They are **shouting** / **smiling**.
5. I am **wearing** / **running** because I'm late for class.
6. She sees her brother. She is **waving** / **looking** to him.

C Complete the sentences. Use the correct form of the verbs in the box. Use each verb only once.

laugh	run	smile	stop	wave
~~look~~	shout	start	watch	wear

1. She's _____*looking*_____ at the man.
2. I'm _____ because I'm happy.
3. She's _____ a jacket.
4. He's _____ because he's mad.
5. We're _____ a movie.
6. They're _____ because the traffic light is red.
7. I'm _____ goodbye to my roommate.
8. He's _____ at the funny TV show.
9. She's _____ to catch the train.
10. I'm _____ a new job tomorrow.

CONVERSATION

A Unscramble the words to make a conversation.

Zara. / going? / How's / it / Hi,

_____

fine. / doing? / How / you / are / I'm

_____

So-so.
up? / What's / Yeah?

_____

I'm / tired. / very

_____

Why?
studying / the / for / English test / I'm / tomorrow.

_____

B Complete the conversations. Use your own ideas.

1. **Miguel:** Hi, Lisa.
   Lisa: _____
   Miguel: I'm all right. How are you?
   Lisa: So-so. _____
   Miguel: _____
   Lisa: I'm _____. I have a dentist appointment tomorrow.
   Miguel: _____

2. **Carlos:** Hi, Ara.
   Ara: _____
   Carlos: I'm fine. _____
   Ara: _____
   Carlos: _____
   Ara: I'm _____. My brother used my car and had an accident.
   Carlos: _____

3. **Shauna:** Hi, Lucas.
   Lucas: _____
   Shauna: I'm kind of tired. _____
   Lucas: Pretty good. _____
   Shauna: I'm happy for you. _____
   Lucas: Sounds good!

What Are You Doing?

GRAMMAR

A Match the questions and answers.

1. Are you studying science?
2. Why are you wearing a sweater?
3. Is your Spanish improving?
4. Where is the bus stopping?
5. Are they traveling more these days?
6. Is your daughter smiling?
7. Why are you running?

a. Yes, she is.
b. No, it isn't.
c. Because I need exercise.
d. No, I'm not.
e. Yes, they are.
f. At Lincoln Street.
g. Because it's cold.

B Complete the conversation. Use the present continuous and contractions where possible.

Paula: So, Jane, what (1.) _____ (you, do) these days?

Jane: I (2.) _____ (work) in an office. And I (3.) _____ (study) computer science in the evening.

Paula: You're really busy!

Jane: That's for sure! And in my free time, I (4.) _____ (learn) Spanish for my vacation. I (5.) _____ (travel) to Mexico in October.

Paula: Wow! What about your brothers? How (6.) _____ (they, do)?

Jane: They (7.) _____ (do) great! Alex (8.) _____ (exercise) at the gym a lot, and Adam (9.) _____ (go) to Pacific University.

C Unscramble the words to make questions.

1. studying / English / is / where / Yuki
   _____

2. to / they / where / this / summer / are / traveling
   _____

3. Sayid / meeting / are / we / when
   _____

4. with / you / are / dinner / having / Megan / when
   _____

D What are they doing now? Write sentences about you, your family, and your friends.

1. _____

2. _____

3. _____

4. _____

B HOW DO YOU FEEL?

VOCABULARY AND GRAMMAR

A Choose the best answer to complete each sentence.

1. I have a test tomorrow. I'm _____.
   a. excited
   b. nervous
   c. bored

2. He's shouting. I think he's _____.
   a. angry
   b. bored
   c. happy

3. My dog is sick. I'm _____.
   a. excited
   b. happy
   c. worried

4. She's sleeping at the movies. She's _____.
   a. afraid
   b. bored
   c. excited

B Complete the sentences with how you feel. Use the words from **A**.

1. I'm traveling by airplane tomorrow. _____.
2. I have a test next week. _____.
3. I'm watching a scary movie. _____.
4. I'm _____. I'm happy.
5. _____. I'm bored.
6. _____. I'm angry.

C Complete the sentences. Use the words in the box. One word is extra.

| her | him | it | me | them | us | you |

1. I like Maria. I see _____ every day.
2. That driver is angry with you and me. She is shouting at _____.
3. You are my best friend. I like _____ a lot.
4. You have my keys. Please give _____ to me.
5. I'm planning a trip to Paris. I'm happy about _____.
6. My son is on vacation. I'm writing a letter to _____.

READING AND WRITING

A Read the email.

Dear students,

I hope you are well and enjoying your break. I am writing because many people are sending me emails about the exams. A lot of you are very (1.) _____, and I understand why. These are important tests, and you're working very hard in class. Many of you are feeling very tired because you're studying all day in the library. I want to help you feel more relaxed, so I'm inviting you to meditation classes every Friday at 1:00 p.m. in the gym. The first one is this Friday.

Some of you may think meditation[1] (2.) _____. Some say sitting in silence for 20 minutes is difficult and makes them angry. That's OK. I just want you to try it, and if you don't (3.) _____ afterward, don't come to the next class.

Meditation helps me think clearly and sleep well after a difficult day. It helps me control my breathing and feel (4.) _____. I believe these classes can teach you how to be (5.) _____ of tests, and, afterward, people usually feel excited about the next class.

So, if you have a fear of tests, or you just get excited about learning new things, please join me. All you need is comfortable clothing and an open mind!

Yours sincerely,

Professor Bisset

[1] **Meditation** is using different ways of thinking and breathing to relax the mind.

B Choose the correct options to complete the email in **A**. Write the letter.

a. feel happy
b. is boring
c. nervous about them
d. less afraid
e. more relaxed

C What are the benefits of meditation? Use information from the article and your own ideas.

_____
_____
_____
_____
_____
_____

D Complete the sentences with object pronouns.

1. My roommate is afraid of dogs, but I like _____.
2. I love talking to my mother. I call _____ every night.
3. Stop! Please don't run so fast. I need to speak to _____.
4. Can you write your name in Korean? I can show _____ how to do it.
5. My driving test is tomorrow. I'm so worried about _____.
6. My brothers didn't clean the kitchen. I'm angry at _____.
7. I'm angry. It's hard for _____ to study with all that loud music.
8. When she speaks Portuguese, she feels nervous. It's difficult for _____.
9. We love yoga. It helps _____ feel relaxed.
10. My uncle is very funny. I always laugh with _____.

E Write about something that makes you feel angry.

_____
_____
_____
_____
_____
_____
_____
_____
_____

3 SHOPPING

A AT THE SUPERMARKET

VOCABULARY

A Unscramble the letters to write the names of food.

1. cei rmeac _____
2. dlsaa _____
3. ygrtou _____
4. chiknce _____
5. gnrdou fbee _____
6. lpapes _____
7. prasge _____
8. tmotaose _____
9. crarots _____
10. fshi _____
11. ttculee _____
12. eschee _____
13. ckea _____
14. ngraoe jciue _____
15. nanaabs _____

B Choose the word that does not belong in each set.

1. apples | ~~french fries~~ | grapes | bananas
2. chips | sugar | cake | fish
3. yogurt | salad | ice cream | butter
4. tea | orange juice | rice | milk
5. cereal | carrots | lettuce | tomato
6. beef | chicken | bread | fish

C Complete the chart.

Foods I Like ☺	Foods that Are OK 😐	Foods I Don't Like ☹

CONVERSATION

A Number the sentences in order to make a conversation.

_____ a. OK. What about frozen food?

_____ b. We need some drinks. Buy soda and juice, please.

_____ c. OK. I'm going to the store. See you later.

__1__ d. I'm making a shopping list for the class party. We have cake. What else do we need?

_____ e. We don't need any. We have some frozen french fries and ground beef.

B Unscramble the words to make a conversation.

1. **Natalia:** what / fridge / have / do / we / in / the
   _____

2. **Pedro:** we / chicken / have / and lettuce, / but / need / we / peppers
   _____

3. **Natalia:** OK. / else / need / we / do / what
   _____

4. **Pedro:** need / we / noodles / and carrots
   _____

5. **Natalia:** do / have / we / breakfast / anything for
   _____

6. **Pedro:** me / think / let
   _____

C Write new conversations. Use the words in the shopping lists.

Barbecue
beef, chips,
french fries, carrots
dessert: grapes, apples

1. **Mario:** _____
   Ellen: _____
   Jim: _____
   Ellen: _____
   Mario: _____

Graduation Party
chicken, fish,
lettuce, tomatoes,
soda, ice cream

2. **Toshi:** _____
   Leo: _____
   Toshi: _____
   Leo: _____
   Toshi: _____

3. **You:** _____
   Your friend: _____
   You: _____
   Your friend: _____
   You: _____

GRAMMAR

A Complete the chart with items from the picture.

Count	Noncount
three apples	grapes

B Complete the sentences with *a*, *an*, or — (if no article is needed).

1. I need to buy ____ new refrigerator.
2. Do you drink coffee with ____ milk?
3. Jose is reading ____ interesting book.
4. I live in ____ old building.
5. Where can we buy ____ bread?
6. There is ____ mountain near my city.
7. Please get ____ soap at the store.
8. Mrs. Yoon is baking ____ cake.
9. Hannah eats ____ sandwich for lunch.
10. Can I have ____ bread, please?

C Rewrite the sentences. Correct the mistake in each one.

1. I'm sorry. I don't have a money with me today.
   I'm sorry. I don't have money with me today.

2. We have tomatoes and lettuces for the salad.
   _____

3. I'll go to the store and buy four rice.
   _____

4. Do we have an soap in the bathroom?
   _____

5. Are there banana on the table?
   _____

6. Do you want a cheese in your sandwich?
   _____

7. We need to buy a milk.
   _____

8. There is egg in the refrigerator.
   _____

B LET'S GO SHOPPING!

VOCABULARY AND GRAMMAR

A Choose the correct words to complete the sentences.

1. I need to **buy** / **sell** some rice for dinner tonight.
2. Can I **go shopping** / **try on** the blue dress, please?
3. How much is it? I don't want to **spend** / **sell** too much money.
4. Can I **return** / **pay** this sweater, please? It's too big.
5. I **sell** / **return** things in my online shop.
6. I want to **go shopping** / **try on**, but it's a holiday so the stores are closed.

B Write the correct words to complete the sentences.

1. There are _____ eggs on the table.
   a. some
   b. any
   c. much
2. I have _____ clothes.
   a. any
   b. much
   c. a lot of
3. There isn't _____ milk in the glass.
   a. some
   b. much
   c. many
4. There aren't _____ students in this class.
   a. some
   b. much
   c. many
5. There isn't _____ salad on the table.
   a. any
   b. some
   c. many
6. There is _____ butter on the bread.
   a. any
   b. some
   c. much

C Write sentences about yourself. Use *some*, *any*, *much*, *many*, or *a lot of*.

1. T-shirts — *I have a lot of T-shirts.*
2. close friends _____
3. jewelry _____
4. books in English _____
5. money _____
6. shoes _____
7. new clothes _____
8. glasses _____

READING AND WRITING

A Read the shopping guide.

SHOPPING GUIDE

metrostore.com

Prices: $$$$$ **Service:** 😊😊😊😊😊

Metrostore.com is a new online store that sells a lot of different products. It's a great place for electronics. There are a lot of cool new cameras, cell phones, and computers. You can buy many things for your house. The clothes are great, too, but the prices aren't great. Everything is very expensive, but the customer service is very helpful and quick to respond.

Gracy's Department Store

Prices: $$ **Service:** 😊😊

Gracy's Department Store has some nice clothes for your parents, but there aren't many things for young people. The prices are quite low. Don't shop for most electronics here—there are just a few tablets, and there aren't any TVs or computers. But the music department is great. It has a good selection of headphones and speakers.

The Little Shop of Sales

Prices: $ **Service:** 😊😊😊

The Little Shop of Sales isn't like most stores. They don't sell new items. Their stuff is "like new" or "gently used." They only sell clothing and furniture. However, you won't find any junk here. If you don't have a lot of spending money, this is the place for you. Come early on Saturday mornings before all the good stuff is gone.

B Read the shopping guide again. Write the name of each store in front of the correct description.

1. _____ A good place for people who like music.

2. _____ A good place to buy electronics.

3. _____ A good place if you don't want to spend a lot of money.

C Choose **T** for *true* or **F** for *false*. Rewrite the false sentences to make them true.

1. The Little Shop of Sales has high prices.   T (F)
   The Little Shop of Sales has low prices.

2. Gracy's has a lot of clothing for young people.   T   F
   _____

3. You can buy a new tablet at the Little Shop of Sales.   T   F
   _____

4. Metrostore.com has a good electronics department.   T   F
   _____

5. Gracy's has low prices.   T   F
   _____

6. Metrostore.com sells used items.   T   F
   _____

D Write items of clothing from your closet in each column.

Count Nouns	Noncount Nouns

E Write a review for a store or website you don't like. Why don't you like it?

_____
_____
_____
_____
_____
_____
_____

4
VACATION

A HOW'S THE WEATHER?

VOCABULARY

A Complete the weather words.

1. w ___ r m
2. w ___ ___ d y
3. h ___ ___
4. c h ___ l ___ ___
5. s ___ n ___ ___
6. r a ___ n ___ ___ g
7. s ___ o w ___ n ___
8. c ___ l ___
9. f ___ e ___ z i ___ g
10. c ___ o ___ d y

B Write words from **A** under the correct images.

1. _____

2. _____

3. _____

4. _____

5. _____

6. _____

C Complete the sentences with words from **A**. There may be more than one possible answer.

1. It's a little _____ outside. You should wear a sweater.
2. It's so _____! I need to drink some water.
3. I love the spring because it's nice and _____ but not too hot.
4. Take an umbrella. It's _____.
5. Be careful, there's so much ice! It's _____ out.
6. It looks _____ today. Maybe it will rain soon.
7. She wears dark glasses when it's _____.
8. It's _____! The weather is good for skiing today.

CONVERSATION

A Unscramble the words to make sentences.

1. should / you / hat. / a / wear

2. OK. / be / but / thanks, / I'll

3. idea. / else? / anything / good

4. we'll / worry. / OK. / don't / be

5. jacket. / shouldn't / wear / a / she

6. ready / trip? / are / for / you / your

7. think / wear / I / jacket. / a / should / don't / you

B Complete the sentences with words from the box.

| idea | raining | should | shouldn't | take | think | wear | will |

1. Tokyo is cold in February, so you should _____ a warm coat with you.
2. Mexico City is very hot in April. I don't _____ you need so many sweaters.
3. Ok, I _____. Thanks for telling me.
4. It's warm outside. You should _____ your new shorts.
5. Good _____. I'll buy some sunscreen.
6. It's _____ today. We should go tomorrow.
7. The weather in the mountains is cool. You _____ buy a warm jacket.
8. It's chilly out. You _____ wear shorts.

C Use the sentences in the box to make a conversation.

~~Are you going?~~	Well, I don't think you should drive.
It's snowing a lot and the roads aren't safe.	Yeah, you're right. I should stay home tonight.
Really? Why not?	Yes, I think so.

Carlos: Tina's having a party tonight.
Chen: *Are you going?*
Carlos: _____
Chen: _____
Carlos: _____
Chen: _____
Carlos: _____

How's the Weather? | 21

GRAMMAR

A Match the sentence halves.

1. Rita loves soccer,
2. She can watch a video,
3. Her computer doesn't work,
4. It's hot in summer,
5. Haru can't drive a car,
6. She has three brothers,
7. She can cook at home,
8. She speaks Spanish,

a. but she doesn't have any sisters.
b. or she can eat at a restaurant.
c. but she doesn't like baseball.
d. so he always takes the bus.
e. but she can't speak French.
f. so she's getting a new one.
g. or she can listen to music.
h. so she always wears T-shirts.

B Rewrite the sentences. Use *or*, *so*, or *but*.

1. It's really cold today. It's very sunny.
   It's really cold today, but it's very sunnny.

2. Should I wear a dress to the party? Should I wear pants?
   _____

3. Abdul likes dogs. He doesn't like cats.
   _____

4. My computer is slow and old. I like it.
   _____

5. We can have fish for dinner. We can have chicken.
   _____

6. It's raining today. We're staying home.
   _____

C Complete the sentences with *or*, *so*, or *but*.

1. It's warm today, _____ it's raining out.
2. Should we visit Lima in May _____ June?
3. It's freezing there, _____ take a warm coat.
4. Filipe loves fish, _____ he hates crab.
5. Should we walk _____ take the subway?
6. Marta has a soccer game on Friday, _____ she is resting today.

D Complete the sentences using *or*, *so*, or *but*. Use your own ideas.

1. I'm studying English, *so, I can get a job in Sydney* _____.
2. My favorite sport is _____.
3. Today, I can _____.
4. I like _____.
5. I have _____.
6. I am _____.

B TAKING A TRIP

VOCABULARY AND GRAMMAR

A Write the words from the box in the table. Some words go with more than one verb.

| photos   shopping   sightseeing   a suitcase   sunglasses   swimming   a ticket   a trip   a vacation |

buy	go	pack	take
		a suitcase	

B Complete the sentences with *buy*, *go*, *pack*, or *take*.

1. Did you _____ your plane tickets online?
2. Remember to _____ a lot of warm clothes for your trip.
3. I always _____ a lot of photos when I visit a new city.
4. You should _____ your suitcase two days before your trip.
5. Hayato wants to _____ a vacation somewhere hot and sunny this year.
6. Olga wants to _____ sightseeing when she visits Rio.
7. My parents _____ a trip to a different national park each summer.
8. You shouldn't _____ swimming in the ocean in winter. It's freezing!

C Choose the correct answers.

1. This is **my / mine** passport.
2. The suitcases are **them / theirs**.
3. **Our / Ours** plane tickets are in my bag.
4. **Whose / Who** sunglasses are these?
5. It's **his / him** car.
6. Is this phone **your / yours**?
7. These shopping bags are **their / theirs**.
8. **My / Mine** shorts are blue.
9. **Their / Theirs** daughter is very tall!

D Complete each sentence with the correct possessive pronoun.

1. I have a new passport. It's _____*mine*_____.
2. You have a big suitcase. It's _____.
3. She has an expensive car. It's _____.
4. He has a ticket. It's _____.
5. We have two kittens. They're _____.
6. They have car keys. They're _____.

Taking a Trip | 23

READING AND WRITING

A Read the article.

Watch the Weather!

Most people plan their vacations very carefully. They think a lot about plane tickets, passports, and places to stay. But they often forget about one important thing—the weather. You should learn about the right time to visit your vacation spot. Here is some information to help you plan your next vacation.

Italy The weather is mostly sunny all year, but it's sometimes cold in winter. April and May are warm and beautiful. From June to September, it's very hot.

It's very hot in Venice, Italy, from June to September.

Australia Summer here is from December to April. It sometimes rains, but the weather is usually very good. In winter, it snows a little in some places, but most of Australia isn't very cold.

Hong Kong The weather is hot here a lot of the year. In July and August, it's sometimes very windy, and there are bad storms. October and November are warm, but in December and January, it gets very chilly sometimes.

Germany From November to April, the weather is cold, cloudy, and snowy. In spring, it's warm, but there's a lot of rain. July and August are usually warm and sunny.

India June to September is monsoon season in many parts of India, like Mumbai and New Delhi. It rains a lot. From November to April, after the rainy season, the weather is nice and cool. In April and May, it gets very hot.

B Choose **T** for *true* or **F** for *false*, according to the article.

1. In Germany, the weather is chilly in spring. T F
2. It rains a lot in India in August. T F
3. It is never chilly in Italy. T F
4. It is usually windy in Hong Kong in November. T F
5. It sometimes snows in Australia. T F
6. In Germany, it's usually rainy in July. T F
7. The summer is the best time to travel to India. T F
8. In Hong Kong, it is chilly most of the year. T F
9. It usually isn't cloudy in Italy. T F
10. Summer is at the same time in Australia and Italy. T F

C For each place, write the best time for a vacation and the reason.

Place	Best Time	Why?
Italy	April and May	The weather is warm and beautiful.
Australia		
Hong Kong		
Germany		
India		

D Write a paragraph giving advice to someone who wants to visit your hometown. Tell the visitor what the weather is like in January, May, August, and October.

E A friend wants to visit you in July. Write a paragraph telling them what they should and shouldn't bring and why.

5 HEROES

A PIONEERS

VOCABULARY

A Choose the best word to complete each sentence.

1. **Educators** / **Pilots** teach people.
2. **Pilots** / **Authors** write books.
3. **Writers** / **Explorers** lead research trips.
4. **Speakers** / **Scientists** give presentations to people.
5. **Presenters** / **Travelers** show and explain things to groups of people.
6. **Researchers** / **Writers** try to find new information.

B Match the words with similar meanings.

1. writer
2. presenter
3. teacher
4. scientist
5. traveler

a. speaker
b. educator
c. author
d. explorer
e. researcher

C Complete the sentences. Use words from **A** and **B**. There may be more than one correct answer.

1. _____ need passports.
2. _____ talk to large groups of people.
3. _____ fly airplanes.
4. _____ work in schools.
5. _____ discover new things.

D Which job is the most interesting to you? Why?

_____
_____
_____
_____
_____

26 | UNIT 5

CONVERSATION

A Read the sentences and agree or disagree. Use expressions from the box and give your reasons.

| I agree. | I think so, too. | Really? I don't think so. | Sorry, but I disagree. |

1. **Your friend:** I think history is a boring subject.
   You: *Really? I don't think so. I think it's fun to learn about the past.*

2. **Your friend:** I think English is a difficult language to learn.
   You: _____

3. **Your friend:** Bill Gates is a great hero.
   You: _____

4. **Your friend:** I think our city is a really boring place.
   You: _____

5. **Your friend:** Everything is very expensive in our country.
   You: _____

6. **Your friend:** Our teacher gives us too much homework!
   You: _____

B Number the sentences in order to make a conversation.

_____ a. Nelson Mandela.
_____ b. I'm writing a paper about a hero.
_____ c. Really? Why is he your choice?
_____ d. Well, he was a great leader who united his country.
_____ e. That's interesting! Who are you writing about?

C Write the names of two people you think are heroes. Then write two conversations about these people.

1. _____   2. _____

1. **You:** _____
   Your friend: _____
   You: _____
   Your friend: _____
   You: _____

2. **You:** _____
   Your friend: _____
   You: _____
   Your friend: _____
   You: _____

GRAMMAR

A Complete the sentences with *was* or *were*.

Alan Turing (1.) _____ a computer scientist. He (2.) _____ born in London over 100 years ago. In 1938, he got his PhD from Princeton University, New Jersey, US. During World War II, he (3.) _____ a code breaker for the British government. Thousands of people (4.) _____ saved because of his work. Turing and his coworkers (5.) _____ heroes. Turing died in 1954.

code breaker: Alan Turing was a code breaker—a person who solves secret messages.

B Rewrite the sentences so they are negative.

1. My grandfather was famous.
   My grandfather wasn't famous.

2. The Baker sisters were explorers.
   _____

3. My aunt was a teacher.
   _____

4. The sky was clear last night.
   _____

5. The children were excited.
   _____

6. I was confused by the first question.
   _____

C Complete the conversations with *was*, *wasn't*, *were*, or *weren't*, and the subject, if necessary.

1. **A:** ____Was____ Jenna in class yesterday?
   B: No, she __wasn't__. She __was__ at home.

2. **A:** _____ Steve and Julia at the beach on Saturday?
   B: No, _____. They _____ at the library.

3. **A:** _____ Carlos at the pool last night?
   B: No, _____. He _____ in his office.

4. **A:** _____ your brother in Los Angeles last year?
   B: Yes, _____.

5. **A:** _____ Mr. and Mrs. Park in California on vacation last week?
   B: No, _____. They _____ in Rome.

B A HELPING HAND

VOCABULARY AND GRAMMAR

A Complete the words in the sentences.

1. My roommate is very g __ n __ __ o __ s. She gives money to people who need it.
2. I ad __ __ __ e nurses so much. They have a difficult but c __ r __ __ g job.
3. Stefan is so f __ __ e n __ l __, and not just with friends but with s __ __ a n g __ r __, too.
4. Don't be so s __ l __ i s __! The food is for everyone to share.
5. My sister is such a w __ r __ person. She often brings the family t __ __ e __ h __ r for parties.
6. My daughter is so h __ l __ f __ __. She always fixes things in the house for me.

B Complete the sentences. Use the simple past.

1. I _____ (like) grapes when I was a kid, but now I don't.
2. The teacher _____ (explain) it to me, so I understand now.
3. I _____ (reply) to her email last night.
4. Pedro _____ (ask) me a difficult question.
5. Your sister _____ (invite) us to her birthday party.
6. Mr. Kano _____ (offer) to pay for everyone's lunch.
7. She _____ (hand) me the fork to mix the milk and eggs.
8. I _____ (try) to call you, but there was no answer.

C Read the information in the chart. Complete it with your own information. Then write sentences about last night.

	Felipe	Chris and Fatima	Vera	You
Study	yes	no	no	
Visit friends	no	yes	yes	
Watch TV	no	no	yes	

1. Felipe _studied last night. He didn't visit friends. He didn't watch TV._
2. Chris and Fatima _____
3. Vera _____
4. I _____

READING AND WRITING

A Read the article.

Harriet Tubman

Harriet Tubman was an African American hero who saved more than 300 slaves[1] in the 1800s. She was brave and generous, and she is an important person in US history.

She was born as a slave in 1820 in Maryland, in the United States. She escaped[2] in 1849 and traveled 90 miles to Philadelphia. After she escaped, she helped others like her. She joined the Underground Railroad. This wasn't a real railroad. It was a network[3] of people who helped slaves escape. She rescued over 300 people, including her own family.

Tubman was also a cook, a nurse, and, later, a spy for the Union army during the American Civil War. With the army, she saved 700 slaves in South Carolina. When the war ended, she cared for former[4] slaves in her home.

Later in life, Tubman didn't have much money. Her friend Sarah H. Bradford, a generous author, admired her. Bradford gave Tubman the money she made from a book she wrote about Tubman. Tubman then helped old people, too. She gave land to a church, which opened The Harriet Tubman Home for the Aged. She died in 1913 at her home in Auburn, New York.

Now, many schools across the United States are named after Harriet Tubman, and teachers tell her story in history classes all over the world.

[1] *Slaves* are people who are forced to work for free.
[2] To *escape* is to run away from a place.
[3] A *network* is a connected group of people or things.
[4] *Former* describes something that used to be.

B Complete the chart about Harriet Tubman with information from the article. Write full sentences. Use the simple past.

Born	
Work	
How she became famous	
Died	

C Complete the paragraph with the simple past of each verb.

Frida Kahlo is a hero to many people in Mexico.
She **(1.)** _____ (be) born in Mexico in 1907.
She **(2.)** _____ (be) a great artist. She
(3.) _____ (marry) Diego Rivera, another artist,
but they **(4.)** _____ (have, not) any children. She
(5.) _____ (paint) many interesting and beautiful
pictures, even though she **(6.)** _____ (study, not)
art. She **(7.)** _____ (use) many ideas from Mexican
culture in her paintings. She **(8.)** _____ (be) also
very brave. After a terrible accident in 1925, her health
(9.) _____ (be, not) very good. But she
(10.) _____ (work) very hard and
(11.) _____ (create) some of the most beautiful
art in the world.

D Write about someone from the past who was brave.

_____
_____
_____
_____
_____
_____
_____
_____
_____
_____
_____
_____
_____
_____
_____
_____

6 THE MIND

A MEMORY

VOCABULARY

A Match the sentence halves.

1. I always forget to
2. It's easy to remember your name
3. I have a bad memory. I forgot
4. I have a good memory. I
5. I recognize you
6. I'm a new student. It's hard to

a. from your photograph.
b. remember where all my classes are.
c. bring my book to class.
d. her email address again.
e. know all of my friends' birthdays.
f. because it's the same as mine.

B Complete the sentences with the words in the box.

| easy to | hard to | have a good | recognize |
| forget | have a bad | memory | |

1. My _____ is full of English vocabulary after studying all day.
2. It is not _____ remember things when you get older.
3. Can you text the address to me, please? I _____ memory.
4. Don't _____ to buy groceries on your way home from work.
5. It's _____ remember everybody's name. There are so many people here.
6. I know how to get there. I _____ memory. Follow me.
7. I'm sorry, I don't _____ you. Did we meet at Sam's party?

C Complete the email with the correct words from the box in **B**.

Dear Zara,

I'm sorry I didn't (1.) _____ you at the subway station last week. I (2.) _____ memory for faces. It was great to talk to you and I'm looking forward to the meeting on Monday about the new project.

Can you send me the notes from the last meeting, please? It's (3.) _____ follow what people are talking about without notes. Do you want to meet for a coffee before the next meeting to talk about your project? There is a nice cafe close to the building where I sometimes go for breakfast. It's very (4.) _____ find.

I hope to see you soon.

P.S.—Don't (5.) _____ to send me the recipe you told me about!

Yours sincerely,

Janika

CONVERSATION

A Unscramble the questions and answers.

1. **Q:** green tea / like / mother / your / does _____
   A: so / think / don't / I _____

2. **Q:** Stefan / explorer / an / is _____
   A: sure / I'm / maybe, / not _____

3. **Q:** is / station / there / subway / near / a / here _____
   A: there / Yes, / is _____

4. **Q:** Australia / from / they / are _____
   A: no, / aren't. / they / they're / South Africa / from _____

B Write responses to the questions. Use degrees of certainty.

1. Does someone in your family have a birthday next month?
   Maybe, I'm not sure.

2. Can you remember your best friend's phone number from memory?
   _____

3. Can you remember all of the addresses where you have lived?
   _____

4. Can you remember the weather on New Year's Day this year?
   _____

5. Can you remember what you ate for dinner last Tuesday?
   _____

6. Is there a movie theater near your school?
   _____

C Write the sentences in order to make a conversation.

> No, really. I forgot where I put it.
> You're kidding.
> Wait, I found it. It was in my coat pocket!
> No, I'm not ready. I can't find my wallet.
> Is it in your car?
> I don't think so. I checked the car.
> OK. Somewhere else then. Please try to remember, Sara!

Alain: *Are you ready for our camping trip?*

Sara: _____

Alain: _____

Sara: _____

Alain: _____

Sara: _____

Alain: _____

Sara: _____

GRAMMAR

A Complete the chart.

Verb	Simple past	Verb	Simple past
come	(1.) _____	know	(11.) _____
do	(2.) _____	make	(12.) _____
drink	(3.) _____	(13.) _____	bought
(4.) _____	ate	ring	(14.) _____
forget	(5.) _____	(15.) _____	sang
(6.) _____	got	(16.) _____	slept
give	(7.) _____	(17.) _____	sold
go	(8.) _____	speak	(18.) _____
(9.) _____	had	understand	(19.) _____
keep	(10.) _____	(20.) _____	said

B Look at Karen's list from yesterday. Write what she did and didn't do.

Friday
1. go to the post office
2. buy food for dinner ✓
3. do my math homework ✓
4. return books to the library
5. get new shoes
6. make dinner for Helena ✓

1. *She didn't go to the post office.*
2. _____
3. _____
4. _____
5. _____
6. _____

C Write sentences. What did you do?

Yesterday

1. _____
2. _____

Last week

3. _____
4. _____

Last year

5. _____
6. _____

B SLEEP

VOCABULARY AND GRAMMAR

A Complete the paragraph with the words in the box.

| asleep | awake | bed | dream | rest | sleep | sleeping | wake |

I like to **(1.)** _____ up early so I can run before breakfast. When I don't

(2.) _____ much the night before, it is hard for me to stay **(3.)** _____

all day.

On days like this, I go to **(4.)** _____ right after dinner. I don't run at night anymore

because it gives me too much energy, and I can't fall **(5.)** _____.

Now, I prefer to read and take a bath to **(6.)** _____ my mind and body in the evening.

I don't usually **(7.)** _____ when I'm asleep, but when I'm not **(8.)** _____

well, I sometimes do.

B Find the mistake in each sentence. Then rewrite the sentences.

1. Did you went to the movie theater last night with your friends?
   _____

2. Where do you go on vacation last year?
   _____

3. I remembered my sunglasses, but I didn't remembered my watch.
   _____

4. Yesterday, I eat toast for breakfast and went to school early.
   _____

5. What do Julio buy at the bookstore?
   _____

C Complete the conversation. There may be more than one correct answer.

Amir: I did something interesting last night.

Ellen: Really? What **(1.)** _____?

Amir: I went to a new restaurant.

Ellen: Oh? Where **(2.)** _____?

Amir: A new Japanese restaurant called Sakura.

Ellen: **(3.)** _____?

Amir: We had fish.

Ellen: **(4.)** _____?

Amir: Yes, I liked it a lot. It was delicious.

Ellen: **(5.)** _____ Japanese tea?

Amir: No, I didn't. I drank coffee.

READING AND WRITING

A Read the article.

Understanding Sleep

Scientists know that the brain is very active when a person is sleeping. There are four stages, or parts, of sleep.

Stage 1 starts after you fall asleep. If there is a noise or a bright light, you wake up very easily. In Stage 2, your brain waves are very slow, and your body gets ready for deep sleep. Stage 3 is deep sleep. It's very difficult to wake up then. Your body rests and grows during this stage.

Stage 4 is when you dream. Your eyes move a lot, and your brain waves are fast. This stage of sleep is very important for your memory. After Stage 4, you wake up a little, and then Stage 1 starts again. We go through the four stages of sleep four or five times every night, so we have many dreams in one night.

How much sleep do you need? The answer depends on your age. Babies should sleep 15 to 16 hours every day. Children and teenagers need nine or ten hours of sleep, but older people only need six to eight hours. If you sleep for only four hours one night, you may just feel tired the next day. But many nights of bad sleep can be bad for your health. People who don't get enough sleep get sick more often. And sleep is very important for learning. It's one reason why students should go to bed early!

B Answer the questions.

1. How many stages of sleep are there? _____
2. When do people dream? _____
3. How many times do we have Stage 1 sleep each night? _____
4. When does your body grow? _____
5. How much sleep do babies need? _____
6. Why should students sleep a lot? _____
7. Look at the last paragraph again. How much sleep should you get? _____
8. Do you get enough sleep? _____

C Match the words from the text with the meanings.

1. active
2. stages
3. rests
4. brain
5. teenagers
6. sick

a. people 13 to 19 years old
b. busy
c. ill
d. the part of your body that controls thinking
e. relaxes
f. steps

D Complete the conversation with the simple past.

A: When (1.) _____ (I / be) eight years old, I went on my first vacation with my family.

B: Where (2.) _____ (you / go) on vacation?

A: Brazil!

B: (3.) _____ (you / enjoy) yourself?

A: Yes, I did. It was fun!

B: How many days (4.) _____ (you / stay) there?

A: (5.) _____ (we / stay) for three days. (6.) _____ (we / go) to the beach and (7.) _____ (we / swim) in the ocean.

B: Do you want to go back again?

A: Sure! (8.) _____ (I / have) a great time.

E You are going to write about a happy memory. Complete the outline with your own ideas.

1. What is your happy memory?

_____

_____

2. What happened?

_____

_____

3. Who was there?

_____

_____

4. What other things make this a happy memory?

_____

_____

F Now write about your happy memory. Use your notes in **E** to help you.

_____

_____

_____

_____

_____

_____

_____

_____

_____

7 CITY LIFE

A MY NEIGHBORHOOD

VOCABULARY

A Complete the words.

1. b u s s t a t i o n
2. d _ _ a r _ m _ n t s _ o _ e
3. g _ _ s _ a t _ o n
4. g r _ _ e _ y s _ _ _ r e
5. h _ i r s _ l o _
6. n i _ _ t c l _ _
7. p _ l _ c _ s _ _ t i o _
8. _ _ b w _ y s _ a _ i _ n
9. h _ a _ t h c _ u b
10. g _ m
11. n _ i l s _ l _ n
12. b _ _ k s _ o r _
13. t _ a i n s t _ t i _ n

B Complete the sentences with words from **A**.

1. There is a big _____ downtown where you can buy things like clothes, toys, and cell phones.
2. My hair is so long, I think it's time to visit the _____.
3. I'm waiting in the _____ for the next train.
4. Let's go to a _____ tonight to dance!
5. The police officer is taking him to the _____.
6. Please buy carrots and potatoes at the _____.
7. I need to go to the _____. My nails look so bad!
8. The car needs gas! Let's stop at the next _____.
9. My sister is exercising at the _____.
10. The bus leaves from the _____ on Washington Street.

C Read the questions. Write where the speaker is. There may be more than one possible answer.

_____ 1. Do you want me to cut it short?
_____ 2. Excuse me. Where can I find the pasta?
_____ 3. Is the bus late?
_____ 4. Do you have yoga classes here?
_____ 5. Excuse me. Do you have this shirt in a smaller size?
_____ 6. When is the next train to Bilbao?

CONVERSATION

A Unscramble the words to make sentences.

1. right / straight / go / and / turn _____
2. Main / on / left / Street / turn _____
3. gas / where's / station / the _____
4. block / of / it's / in / middle / the / the _____
5. First Avenue / one / yes, / there's / on _____

B Look at the map and complete the conversations. Start at the X for Conversation 5.

1. gas station
2. police station
3. Mina's Coffee Shop
4. library
5. Kim's Nail Salon
6. grocery store
7. A.C's Health Club
8. bookstore

1. **A:** Is there a coffee shop around here?
   B: Yes. Mina's Coffee Shop is on *the corner of Washington Street and Fifth Avenue*.

2. **A:** Excuse me. Where's the grocery store?
   B: It's on the _____.

3. **A:** Where's A.C's Health Club?
   B: It's on _____. It's in the middle _____.

4. **A:** Is there a police station near here?
   B: Yes, it's on _____.

5. **A:** How do I get to the library?
   B: Go straight, turn right on Washington Street. It's _____.

C Now complete the conversation about your neighborhood.

Visitor: Excuse me. Is there a coffee shop near here?
You: _____

Visitor: And is there a bank or an ATM?
You: _____

Visitor: How about a bookstore?
You: _____

GRAMMAR

A Look at the map. Answer the questions. Use the prepositions in parentheses.

1. Where is the police station? (on) *It's on Park Avenue.*
2. Where is the supermarket? (on) _____
3. Where is the gym? (across from) _____
4. Where is the movie theater? (on, next to) _____
5. Where is the language school? (on, corner) _____
6. Where is Westlake Avenue? (between) _____
7. Where is the bus stop? (next to) _____

B Write two sentences for each place. Use *across from*, *next to*, *in front of*, *behind*, or *between*.

1. Where is your house?
   _____
   _____

2. Where is your school?
   _____
   _____

3. Where is your favorite restaurant?
   _____
   _____

4. Where is your best friend's house?
   _____
   _____

5. Where is the local gym?
   _____
   _____

B IN THE CITY

VOCABULARY AND GRAMMAR

A Complete the sentences with the words in the box.

| delays | heavy | journey | light | passengers | pollution | transportation system |

1. The _____ in this city is terrible. The buses are always late, and the subway trains are dirty.
2. Don't go that way, there is _____ traffic on the highway.
3. He drives to work at 5:30 a.m., when the traffic is _____.
4. I take the bus and then walk for ten minutes on my _____ to the office.
5. There are fewer _____ on the subway on Sunday morning.
6. The air _____ in the city is very bad, so I wear a mask.
7. There are _____ on the subway this morning, so let's walk.

B Choose the correct forms.

1. Air travel **pollutes** / **pollution** the planet.
2. Don't swim in the river, it is very **polluted** / **pollute**.
3. The government needs to do something about **pollution** / **polluted** from factories.
4. Heavy traffic causes a lot of **pollute** / **pollution**.
5. We stopped driving that car because it **polluted** / **pollute** the air so much.

C Match the sentence halves.

1. How many students
2. How much air
3. How many rainy
4. How much traffic
5. How much rice
6. How many bookstores

a. is there in that box?
b. days are there in spring?
c. pollution is there in Kuala Lumpur?
d. are there in your town?
e. are there in this class?
f. is there on the roads?

D Complete the questions with *How much* or *How many*. Then write the answers in your notebook for your town or city.

1. _____ people are there?
2. _____ traffic is there?
3. _____ pollution is there?
4. _____ parks are there?
5. _____ public transportation is there?
6. _____ good restaurants are there?

READING AND WRITING

A Read the article.

TRAVEL GUIDE

Choosing a City

Istanbul, Turkey
Istanbul is a very special city—one part is in Europe, and the other part is in Asia. About 15 million people live there. Visitors love Istanbul because it has many beautiful, old buildings, and the food is great. At night, the seafood restaurants are very popular. And everything in Istanbul is very affordable for visitors. Traffic is a problem in the city because there are too many cars for the old streets. There are also subways, trains, and buses, and some people take boats to go between the European side and the Asian side. The weather is very good in summer, but in winter it's sometimes very cold.

Vancouver, Canada
Vancouver is one of the most beautiful cities in the world. It's near the mountains and the ocean, and there are many great parks where you can walk, ride a bicycle, or just relax. The city has good public transportation with buses and fast trains that go everywhere. There are about 630,000 people in Vancouver, but it's a very clean city, and there's not much pollution. But, there are two bad points—prices there are very high, and the weather is not very good. Vancouver is famous for rain! But there are many good museums for those rainy days, and in the evening, the city has great restaurants and nightclubs to visit.

B Match the words from the article with the meanings.

1. special
2. seafood
3. popular
4. affordable
5. museums
6. points
7. famous

a. not expensive
b. places to see interesting things (art, for example)
c. things
d. fish and other sea animals you can eat
e. liked by many
f. different
g. known by many

C Find information about the two cities and write it in the chart.

	Istanbul	Vancouver
Location		
Population		
Weather		
Transportation		
Cost		

D Read the paragraph. Identify the eight spelling mistakes. Rewrite the words correctly on the lines below.

Singapore is a great city for a vacation. There are alot of interesting things to see. You can visit Chinatown and Little India and go shopping on Orchard Road. Singapore also has many good restarants. There are some great beaches for swimming naer the city, and the parks are really beutiful. The city has very good public transportion. You can take a bus, trane, or subway. It's a safe city. It's also a clean city. There isn't much polution. The only problem is that Singapore is expensiev.

1. _____
2. _____
3. _____
4. _____
5. _____
6. _____
7. _____
8. _____

E Write about a city you think is good for a vacation.

_____
_____
_____
_____
_____
_____
_____
_____

ALL ABOUT YOU

A SPORTS

VOCABULARY

A Unscramble the letters to write the names of sports.

1. ckro nglcimbi _____
2. blsktlaeba _____
3. bikngi _____
4. fldie hckoye _____
5. skteabdringoa _____

6. sccreo _____
7. ingfsru _____
8. smiwmngi _____
9. nngrnui _____
10. snteni _____

B Complete the chart with the words from **A**. Add other sports you know.

I like it. ☺	It's OK. 😐	I don't like it. ☹

C Complete the sentences with *play* or *go*. Use the correct verb form.

1. Ramon and Felipe _____ basketball every Saturday.
2. It's cold, so we can't _____ swimming at the beach.
3. Gianna _____ field hockey for her school team.
4. Do you _____ tennis in the park?
5. People often _____ skateboarding in the park.
6. John _____ rock climbing with his friends every weekend.
7. Let's _____ baseball.
8. I usually _____ running in the morning.
9. She always _____ surfing at the beach on the weekends.
10. Eric _____ soccer for the school team.

CONVERSATION

A Unscramble the words to make conversations. Add punctuation where necessary.

1. **A:** soccer / do / play / want / you / to _____
   B: I'd / love / sure / to _____
2. **A:** want / you / to / do / go / with / running / me _____
   B: thanks / can't / but / I _____
3. **A:** go / you / do / to / want / swimming _____
   B: I'd / to / busy / love / I'm / but _____

B Number the sentences in order to make a conversation.

_____ a. That sounds fun! Where?
_____ b. Great, I'll text you on Friday night.
_____ c. At Hamilton Beach. Do you want to come?
_____ d. That's OK. We're going next weekend, too. Would you like to come then?
_____ e. I'd love to, but I need to take care of my younger sister tomorrow.
_____ f. Sure, sounds good!
_____ g. Hi, Amira. I'm going surfing with some friends tomorrow.

C Write new conversations using the words.

1. swimming / tomorrow / pool / in Center Park
   A: _____
   B: _____
   A: _____
   B: Sure, _____

2. baseball / tonight / a big test tomorrow
   A: _____
   B: _____
   A: _____
   B: Sorry, _____

3. (your ideas)
   A: _____
   B: _____
   A: _____
   B: Sure, _____

4. (your ideas)
   A: _____
   B: _____
   A: _____
   B: Sorry, _____

Sports | 45

GRAMMAR

A Draw lines to match the words.

1. I need	to tell	the park.
2. They want	to swim	music.
3. She wants	biking in	my driving test.
4. They like	to meet	home instead.
5. Sorry, I forgot	to pass	car.
6. I love	rock	you earlier.
7. I learned	to stay	at the local pool.
8. We decided	a new	at the subway station.

B Rewrite each sentence. Correct one mistake in each one.

1. I expect winning the game tonight.
_____

2. Where did you learn play tennis?
_____

3. She enjoys to swimming.
_____

4. They plan play field hockey this evening.
_____

5. They love to movies.
_____

C Complete the sentences with words from the box.

| biking | forget | learn | to go | to study |
| driving | hate | like | to play | to surf |

1. They love _____ together, and they have the same kind of bicycle.
2. I _____ to go swimming when the water is cold.
3. I need _____ or I'll fail the exam.
4. I _____ to drive when the traffic is light.
5. She wants to _____ how to play tennis.
6. I love _____ on these quiet roads.
7. Some people love _____ in the Pacific Ocean.
8. They want _____ rock climbing this weekend.
9. We prefer _____ soccer in the evening.
10. I always _____ to bring my gym clothes.

B PERSONALITY

VOCABULARY AND GRAMMAR

A Match the opposites.

1. neat
2. ambitious
3. careful
4. shy

a. talkative
b. careless
c. messy
d. easy-going

B Complete the sentences with the words from **A**.

1. My sister is kind of _____. Her clothes are always on her bedroom floor.
2. I'm a little _____. I get nervous when people I don't know talk to me.
3. She is very _____ when she goes rock climbing. She always checks the safety equipment twice.
4. Ana is so _____! I think I know everything about her life after speaking to her!
5. Don't be _____. Wear a helmet when you go biking.
6. Claude is so _____. He doesn't worry about anything.
7. My father is really _____. He organizes his books in alphabetical order.
8. Zara is very _____. She wants to study law at Harvard University!

C Write a description of a friend. Use at least four adjectives from **B**.

_____
_____
_____
_____

D Write the time expressions in order of frequency. Then write a sentence for each one.

| all the time | every Sunday | never | twice a month |
| every day | hardly ever | once in a while | |

1. *all the time* — *I wear glasses all the time.*
2. _____ _____
3. _____ _____
4. _____ _____
5. _____ _____
6. _____ _____
7. _____ _____

READING AND WRITING

A Read the article.

The Right Personality

Do you have the right personality for these jobs?
We asked some people what it takes to be successful in their field.

Don Pierce, movie star
A good actor wants to succeed. Most laid-back actors never become famous. Successful actors also get to know the right people in Hollywood. In addition, they are able to think creatively, and they understand people very well. That helps them understand the different characters they play on stage and in movies.

Dr. Janice Little, doctor and author
The most important thing a good doctor can do is be a good listener. You have to understand people and their problems. A good doctor likes to solve problems and always wants to help their patients. And you can't be careless—you should always be careful. Sometimes the first answer you think of isn't the right answer.

Daniel Vasquez, president of a large corporation
To be a success in business, you have to work well with groups of people. At the same time, you need to have strong opinions and be able to explain your opinions clearly. Good businesspeople are able to make quick decisions and try new ideas. They are very organized and they work very long hours.

B Read the paragraphs in the article to find the words that match the meanings below.

Paragraph 1:

1. _____ do well

2. _____ a place in the US famous for movies

3. _____ The place where actors act in front of an audience.

Paragraph 2:

4. _____ know about

5. _____ make better / correct

6. _____ people who doctors take care of

Paragraph 3:

7. _____ Things you believe, or think, are correct.

8. _____ talk about something to help people understand it

9. _____ neat and careful

C According to the article, which things are important for each job?

It's important to . . .	Actor	Doctor	Businessperson
1. be a good listener.		X	
2. be ambitious.			
3. be creative.			
4. understand people.			
5. be careful.			
6. have strong opinions.			
7. want to help people.			
8. be organized.			
9. work well with people.			

D Complete the paragraph. Use the words in the box.

| ambitious | careful | easy-going | organized | shy |

A good athlete is **(1.)** _____. He or she must really want to win! Athletes must also be **(2.)** _____ because their job can be stressful. Progress doesn't always come quickly. Being **(3.)** _____ is also important. There's nothing worse than a player who can't find his or her equipment. Although many athletes are quite talkative, some of them have a **(4.)** _____ side as well. They don't want everyone to know everything about them. The best athletes are also **(5.)** _____. They know that just one careless mistake could cost the whole team an important win!

E What makes a good teacher? Write a paragraph with your ideas.

_____

_____

_____

_____

_____

_____

_____

CHANGE

A PERSONAL HABITS

VOCABULARY

A Complete the chart with the habits from the box. Use your own opinion.

| being late | drinking coffee | napping |
| daydreaming | eating junk food | spending hours online |

Good Habits	Bad Habits

B Match the sentence halves.

1. Many people fail to
2. I need to build
3. She wants to make a
4. Biting your
5. It's so annoying
6. It bothers me when I'm talking
7. I have a habit of daydreaming
8. Drinking tea with a lot of

a. that they're always late.
b. change in her life.
c. break bad habits.
d. good study habits.
e. to you and you look at your phone.
f. in math class.
g. sugar is an unhealthy habit.
h. finger nails is a bad habit.

C What do you want to change about your life? Write five complete sentences.

1. _____
2. _____
3. _____
4. _____
5. _____

CONVERSATION

A Use the sentences in the box to make a conversation.

Do you need it today?	Thanks a lot!
Oh, no! I don't have my book.	Yes, I have class at 10:00. Can I borrow yours?
Sure. No problem.	

A: _____
B: _____
A: _____
B: _____
A: _____

B Unscramble the words to make sentences. Add additional punctuation where necessary.

1. borrow / I / your / can / dictionary? _____
2. go / you / of course / here _____
3. tomorrow? / you / bring / it / could _____
4. but / I / I'm / don't / cash / sorry / have _____
5. your / could / coat? / borrow / I _____
6. no / sure / problem _____
7. here / certainly / is / it _____
8. need to / use it / sorry / I / but _____

C Write new conversations making and responding to requests.

1. cell phone / call my mother

   A: _____
   B: _____
   A: _____
   B: _____
   A: _____

2. (your idea)

   A: _____
   B: _____
   A: _____
   B: _____
   A: _____

GRAMMAR

A Write what each person *likes to* do and what they *would like to* do.

1. Tim / use computers, be a web designer
   Tim likes to use computers. He'd like to be a web designer.

2. Barbara / draw, go to art school
   _____

3. Luis / travel, practice his English in other countries
   _____

4. Maria / talk to people, work in a coffee shop
   _____

5. Nerea / exercise, be a personal trainer
   _____

6. Marcus / play guitar, join a band
   _____

7. you / ?
   _____

B Complete each sentence with *like to* or *would like to*.

1. We always go to France on vacation. Next year, I _____ go to Croatia.
2. When I get up, I always _____ drink coffee and read the newspaper.
3. Myoung-Hee _____ study English in Canada this summer.
4. Jeff _____ have a big dog, but he lives in a very small apartment.
5. I _____ visit my grandmother because she always cooks a big dinner for me.
6. Francisco doesn't like his work. He _____ get a new job.

C Answer the questions with your own ideas in your notebook. Write complete sentences.

1. What do you like to do in the evening?
2. What would you like to do this evening?
3. What do you like to do on vacation?
4. What would you like to do on your next vacation?
5. What do you like to do in English class?
6. What would you like to do next time in English class?
7. What do you like to do when it's cold outside?
8. What would you like to do next summer?

B BREAKING THE PLASTIC HABIT

VOCABULARY AND GRAMMAR

A Complete the sentences with the words in the box. Use each word only once.

| bags | bottles | cups | goal | million | millions | plastic | recycle | reuse | straw | takes |

1. We all need to _____ more instead of throwing everything in the trash.
2. Australians throw away almost three _____ paper coffee _____ every day.
3. Did you know _____ water _____ can be recycled into T-shirts?
4. Don't throw that away! It _____ 450 years for plastic waste to decompose.
5. We throw away _____ of tons of plastic every year.
6. We don't sell plastic _____ in this grocery store. You need to bring one you can _____ with you.
7. I try not to use a _____ when I buy iced coffee.
8. Her _____ this year is to use less plastic.

B What do you recycle and how do you do it?

_____
_____
_____
_____
_____
_____

C Complete the chart for you. Then write about each person's future plans.

	Fatima	Ken	Dan and Marta	You
Move to another city	no	yes	no	
Travel	yes	no	yes	
Start a business	yes	no	no	

1. What is Fatima going to do in the future?
   She is going to travel and start a business. She isn't going to move to another city.

2. What is Ken going to do in the future?
   _____
   _____

3. What are Dan and Marta going to do in the future?
   _____
   _____

4. What are you going to do in the future?
   _____
   _____

READING AND WRITING

A Read the article.

Creative Recycling

When we think about recycling, we usually think of throwing plastic bottles or paper cups into a recycling bin. But do you ever think about what happens to those items afterwards? You may be surprised. Here are three examples of creative recycling:

The Mall of America in Minnesota, US, has 40 million visitors each year and 50 restaurants. That means a lot of waste. But America's biggest shopping center doesn't just throw it out. In fact, the mall recycles 240 tons of food waste by giving it all to a local pig farm!

A bedroom in the cockpit of JumboStay Airplane Hostel

When you walk the streets of Manila, Philippines, or Dakar, Senegal, at night, you may see something surprising. An organization called Liter of Light takes plastic bottles and reuses them as solar lights. The idea helps with two problems. The first is plastic waste and the second is bad lighting in homes. Liter of Light puts water and bleach in a plastic bottle and attaches it to the roof of a house. The sunlight hits the water and when it gets dark, the bottle works just like a 50-watt light bulb.

Recycling isn't possible only with small items. In Arlanda, Sweden, an old airplane sat outside the local airport for years. One day, an ambitious businessman had an idea for how to solve the problem of hotels near the airport being too expensive. He bought the airplane and turned it into JumboStay, a hostel with 25 rooms. One night at the hostel costs just $45, and you can even have a coffee in the airplane's cafe when you wake up.

So, next time you recycle something, think about how you can reuse it. Who knows, maybe you will have an idea that can help the planet in a creative way.

B Choose **T** for *true* or **F** for *false*.

1. The Mall of America has 40 million visitors every year.   T   F
2. The Mall of America gets food for their restaurants from a local farm.   T   F
3. Liter of Light uses glass bottles to make lights.   T   F
4. Liter of Light's lights use power from the sun.   T   F
5. You can only recycle small items.   T   F
6. The airplane hostel is expensive.   T   F

C Read and complete the email with vocabulary from Lesson A.

Dear Mom,

I hope you and Dad are well. My exams went well, but I'm not so good. My new roommate is so annoying! She has a **(1.)** h_____ of playing loud music late at night when I am trying to study. In fact, she has a lot of **(2.)** b_____ habits. For example, she always leaves the fridge door open, and she is so messy! She eats a lot of junk food, which is such an **(3.)** un_____ habit. She also watches TV all day!

I told her these things **(4.)** b_____ me and she said she will try to be more careful.

Sorry, I **(5.)** h_____ a **(6.)** h_____ of complaining to you in emails. I need to be more positive.

I will call you on Tuesday.

Lots of love,

Nerea

D Write about some bad or unhealthy habits you have.

E Now write about your plans to change your bad habits.

Breaking the Plastic Habit | 55

10 HEALTH

A THE BODY

VOCABULARY

A Unscramble the letters to write parts of the body.

1. danh _____
2. tsehc _____
3. mar _____
4. knec _____
5. deah _____

6. humto _____
7. ckba _____
8. mchstoa _____
9. caef _____
10. drelshou _____

B Look at the photo. Write the number next to each body part.

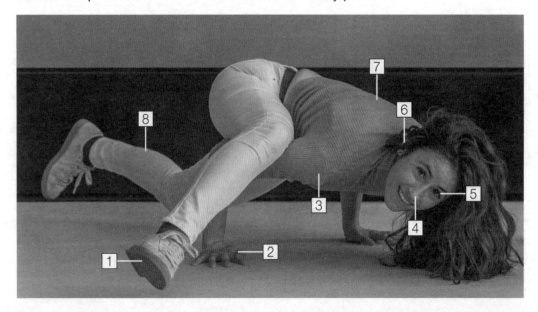

a. ____ back
b. ____ ear
c. ____ eye
d. ____ foot
e. ____ hand
f. ____ leg
g. ____ nose
h. ____ shoulder

C Match the sentence halves.

1. Cover your eyes so
2. Point to where it
3. Rub the cream
4. We stand on
5. This T-shirt is too short,
6. My legs are too
7. It is difficult to buy shoes

a. hurts on your leg.
b. our feet.
c. because I have small feet.
d. so, I need a bigger size.
e. you can't see anything.
f. on your hands.
g. long for these pants.

56 | UNIT 10

CONVERSATION

A Write the sentences in order to make a conversation.

Are you OK?	No. I don't feel well.
I can't meet you tonight.	Oh, sorry to hear that. Get some rest, and I'll call you in the morning.
I have a headache, and I feel really tired.	What's the matter?

Mario: Hi, Tina. Sorry, but _____.

Tina: _____

Mario: _____

Tina: _____

Mario: _____

Tina: _____

B Unscramble the words to complete the conversation. Add additional punctuation where necessary.

Irina: Hi, Dan. How's it going?

Dan: Hi, / OK / I'm / are / for / ready / the party? / you _____

Irina: No. That's why I'm calling. I can't go.

Dan: really? / not? / why _____

Irina: stomach / hurts / my _____

Dan: sorry / to / no / hear / that / oh _____

Irina: I'm sorry. I know you wanted me to give you a ride.

Dan: worry / about / don't / it _____

Irina: Thanks for understanding.

Dan: care / take _____

C Write two new conversations. Give your own advice.

1. (sore throat / can't talk)

   A: _____
   B: _____
   A: _____
   B: _____
   A: _____
   B: _____

2. (your own idea)

   A: _____
   B: _____
   A: _____
   B: _____
   A: _____
   B: _____

GRAMMAR

A Match the sentence halves to make imperatives.

1. Close
2. Don't forget
3. Don't
4. Stay
5. Don't move your
6. Go
7. Don't turn
8. Take

a. left.
b. calm.
c. your eyes.
d. an aspirin.
e. arms or legs.
f. panic.
g. to do it.
h. straight.

B Write advice. Use imperatives.

1. I love coffee, but I can't sleep at night.
   Don't drink coffee in the afternoon or at night.

2. My back hurts when I wake up in the morning.
   _____

3. I have a sore throat.
   _____

4. I'm a teacher. My feet hurt after work every day.
   _____

5. I have a terrible cough.
   _____

6. I want to quit smoking.
   _____

C Complete the tips with the correct verbs.

TIPS FOR HEALTHY LIVING

1. _____ lots of water.
2. _____ so much junk food.
3. _____ to the gym before or after work.
4. _____ for eight hours each night.
5. _____ to take vitamins in the morning.
6. _____ fresh fruits and vegetables at the grocery store.

B STRESS

VOCABULARY AND GRAMMAR

A Complete the sentences. Use the words in the box.

| anxiety | focus | full | low | stressed | stressful |

1. When I'm _____ on energy, I take a cold shower and drink a cup of green tea.
2. I always go to my meditation class. It helps me _____.
3. Mr. Kwan feels _____. His plane is late, and he has an important meeting in two hours.
4. I'm so _____ of energy. I can't sleep!
5. Being a nurse can be a very _____ job.
6. Exams are a cause of _____ for a lot of college students.

B Write sentences with *when*.

1. read a good book / have free time

   I read a good book when I have free time. / When I have free time, I read a good book.

2. study for six hours / feel exhausted

   _____

3. talk to my friend Anna / have a problem

   _____

4. go on vacation / sleep very late

   _____

5. feel healthy / exercise every day

   _____

6. take aspirin / have a headache

   _____

C Complete the sentences with your own ideas.

1. When I have a test, _____.
2. When I get up very early, _____.
3. When I feel stressed, _____.
4. When I have a lot of energy, _____.
5. When I'm low on energy, _____.
6. When I have anxiety, _____.
7. When I can't sleep, _____.

Stress | 59

READING AND WRITING

A Read the article.

Home Remedies

A long time ago when people were sick, they didn't go to the doctor, and they didn't buy medicine from the drugstore. Instead, they used home remedies—medicine made from things at home. Today, many people like to use these ways to feel better because they are cheap and easy to use. Here are some old home remedies from the United States.

1. _____

- Don't eat dinner late at night. Have a small, light dinner early in the evening.
- Eat a salad with lettuce for dinner. It helps with anxiety.
- Eat raw onions to help you sleep.

2. _____

- Cook an onion and put the hot onion on your ear.
- Put some salt in a bag, heat the bag, and put it on the side of your head.
- Put warm oil in your ear.

3. _____

- Don't eat very cold food, like ice cream.
- Lie down and close your eyes. Breathe calmly, and don't think about anything.
- Put a hot cloth on your head, above your eyes.

4. _____

- Eat a lot of yogurt to help your stomach work better.
- Drink tea made from ginger, peppermint, or chamomile plants.
- Don't drink a lot of black tea or coffee.

B Write the correct subtitle for each section (1–4) of the article in **A**. There is one extra subtitle.

When you have a headache

When your feet hurt

When you have stomach problems

When your ear hurts

When you have sleep problems

C Complete the paragraph with the words in the box.

| cook | don't | drink | eat | go | stay | take |

We have many home remedies for coughs in my country. When you have a cough,

(1.) _____ a very hot bath.

(2.) _____ tea with honey and lemon. (3.) _____ exercise because that makes coughs worse.

(4.) _____ warm and

(5.) _____ to bed if the weather is cold. (6.) _____ an egg and

(7.) _____ it while it is still warm.

My grandmother always uses these home remedies.

People drink tea to help with a sore throat caused by a cough.

D Complete the first part of each sentence, beginning with *When*. Use your own ideas.

1. _____ I drink tea or coffee.
2. _____ I go for a walk.
3. _____ I listen to loud music.
4. _____ I talk to my parents.
5. _____ I take a shower.
6. _____ I study hard.

E Write about a home remedy you know about. Or go online and research one.

_____
_____
_____
_____
_____
_____
_____
_____
_____
_____

Stress | 61

11

ACHIEVEMENT

A TALENTED PEOPLE

VOCABULARY

A Unscramble the letters to make words.

1. tlnate _____
2. tlnatede _____
3. ssccsue _____
4. flussccsue _____
5. ccsuede _____
6. gdoo ta _____
7. spciale blityai _____
8. crticepa _____

B Put the words from **A** in the correct columns.

Noun	Verb	Adjective
		good at

C Complete the sentences with the words from **A**.

1. Athletes need to _____ a lot if they want to _____.
2. That is a beautiful painting! You're a very _____ artist.
3. Itsuki is now the boss of his own company. He's very _____.
4. My sister plays the piano and violin very well. She has so much _____.
5. I'm not very _____ soccer, but I'm an OK tennis player.
6. She has a _____. She can solve very difficult math problems, and she is only five years old!
7. I haven't had much _____ with learning Mandarin.

D Use the given words to write questions. Then write answers using your own ideas.

1. **Q:** she / talent — *Does she have talent?*
   A: (your idea) — *Yes. She plays the piano really well.*
2. **Q:** he / natural ability _____
   A: _____
3. **Q:** the site / get / many hits _____
   A: _____
4. **Q:** they / talented _____
   A: _____

62 | UNIT 11

CONVERSATION

A Match the sentence halves to make compliments.

1. You play guitar
2. This cake
3. Great
4. I like this
5. You're a

a. is amazing.
b. food a lot.
c. great singer.
d. really well.
e. job!

B Write compliments for each situation.

1. Your friend is wearing a new jacket.
   _____

2. Your classmate is singing, and it sounds great.
   _____

3. Your friend cooks a delicious dinner for you.
   _____

4. You see your neighbor's beautiful garden.
   _____

5. Your sister paints a pretty picture.
   _____

C Answer the compliments and add information.

1. That's a great shirt.
   Thanks. I got it at Metro Department Store.

2. Your dog is really cute.
   _____

3. You speak English very well.
   _____

4. Your story was really funny.
   _____

5. Those are cool sunglasses.
   _____

6. I like your new haircut.
   _____

7. Your speech was so interesting.
   _____

8. You're such a good tennis player.
   _____

Talented People | 63

GRAMMAR

A Write sentences about the information in the chart. Follow the example.

	Swim	Cook	Speak English
Yoshi (10 years ago)	✓	✗	✗
Yoshi (now)	✓	✓	✗
Estela (10 years ago)	✗	✗	✗
Estela (now)	✓	✗	✓
You (10 years ago)			
You (now)			
✓ = yes ✗ = no			

Yoshi

1. a. He _could swim when he was ten_. b. He _can swim now_.
2. a. He _____ cook when he was ten. b. He _____ now.
3. a. He _____ when he was ten. b. He _____ now.

Estela

4. a. She _____. b. She _____ now.
5. a. She _____. b. She _____ now.
6. a. She _____. b. She _____ now.

You

7. a. I _____. b. I _____ now.
8. a. I _____. b. I _____ now.
9. a. I _____. b. I _____ now.

B Write *can* or *could* to complete each sentence.

1. They _____ both swim when they were five.
2. _____ you drive a car?
3. I _____ hike every weekend when I lived near the mountains.
4. _____ you ride a bike when you were four years old?
5. I _____ speak English well now.
6. She _____ speak Thai when she was a child, but she doesn't remember much now.

C Write the questions to the answers below.

1. A: _____ B: Raul can't speak French.
2. A: _____ B: Nia couldn't swim when she was two.
3. A: _____ B: Lola can make music videos.
4. A: _____ B: Kien could walk when he was seven months old.
5. A: _____ B: Julia can cook paella.

RISK

VOCABULARY AND GRAMMAR

A Complete the paragraph with the words in the box.

| afraid | brave | curious | dangerous | difficult | safe | take |

When I was young, I was **(1.)** _____ of everything! Dogs, heights, spiders, the dark—everything! Now I'm older, and I'm more confident. I am **(2.)** _____ about activities that scared me when I was a boy, and I want to try new things. Last year, I decided to be **(3.)** _____ and do something risky. When my friend told me he was going to climb Mount Fitz Roy, a mountain on the border of Argentina and Chile, I decided to join him. It was time to **(4.)** _____ a chance. It was a **(5.)** _____ climb, and I needed to exercise a lot before I went. It can be **(6.)** _____, too, but my friend is a very **(7.)** _____ person. He always checked that the weather was good before we climbed, and he had all of the best safety equipment.

B Write *because* or *so* to complete each sentence.

1. It was cold, _____ I shut the door.
2. We don't like them _____ they are rude.
3. The water was beautiful, _____ they went swimming.
4. I'll be home late _____ I have a lot of work to do.
5. She failed her exam, _____ she's studying for it again.
6. Felipe is sick, _____ he isn't coming to class today.
7. Anna can't come to dinner _____ it's her mother's birthday.
8. My office is far away, _____ I need to leave the house early.

C Rewrite the sentences. Change the word *so* to *because*, or change the word *because* to *so*.

1. Karen can't drive because she is only 12 years old.
   Karen is only 12 years old, so she can't drive.

2. I was tired, so I went to bed.
   _____

3. We went out to eat because it was my birthday.
   _____

4. The test is tomorrow, so we should study now.
   _____

5. I will leave early because I don't want to be late.
   _____

6. The movie was boring, so I left.
   _____

READING AND WRITING

A Read the article.

Amazing Chefs: Flynn McGarry

Flynn McGarry is an amazing chef. He works very long hours every week, grows his own food for the dishes he creates, and has cooked for the White House. A lot of famous newspapers and magazines have published articles about him. He has spoken at a world famous conference, and he appears on news and talk shows. People come from all over the United States to try his food.

Well, what's unusual about that?

Flynn opened his first pop-up restaurant at sixteen years old. He was only ten when he began cooking after school, and only twelve when he began serving dinners to customers at his family's home in California. He called his monthly supper club Eureka. When he started it, people paid $160 each to try his tasting menu. He did school work in his free time, but spent most of his days trying new recipes or learning from other chefs around the country.

When Flynn isn't in the kitchen, he's likely eating at a favorite restaurant or posting photos of meals for his followers on social media. The videos his mother put online years ago have tens of thousands of hits.

Flynn opened his own restaurant, Gem, in 2018 in New York City, but some people said he was still too young. Because he started working so early, some think he missed out on his childhood. But Flynn doesn't feel that way. Every day, he's excited to do something he loves.

B Choose **T** for *true* or **F** for *false*. Rewrite the false sentences to make them true.

1. Flynn is successful because he grows his own food. T F

_____

2. He started cooking when he was 10. T F

_____

3. Flynn posted videos online. T F

_____

4. Flynn is unhappy that he missed out on his childhood. T F

_____

5. Flynn works a lot. T F

_____

C Read about an achievement. Identify the eight spelling and grammar mistakes. Rewrite the misspelled words and correct the grammar mistakes on the lines below.

When I was an elementary school student, I started to play soccer for my scool team. At first, I was afrad I wouldn't be as good as the other players. My father told me to be brave and that I could stop if it was too dificult. After our first few games, the coach told me to try playing in goal so I was tall. After a few months, he told me I had a lot of talnt. He said I should try to become a professional soccer player! It was the first thing I was really good it. I wanted to play for a famous team one day because I practiced very hard. Finally, I got a chance to play for the Manchester City youth team! My coach and my parents are very proud of my sucess.

1. _____
2. _____
3. _____
4. _____
5. _____
6. _____
7. _____
8. _____

D Write about someone who achieved success when they were young.

_____
_____
_____
_____
_____
_____
_____
_____
_____
_____
_____
_____

AT THE MOVIES

A WHAT'S PLAYING?

VOCABULARY

A Complete the sentences. Use the words in the box.

| action | classic movies | documentaries | dramas | horror | romantic comedies | science fiction |

1. People usually fall in love in _____.
2. Many _____ movies are about the future.
3. Good, old movies are often called _____.
4. _____ are serious films that make you think.
5. _____ movies often have car chases and fights.
6. Movies that scare people are called _____ movies.
7. _____ are always about real people, places, or things.

B Write the type of movie from the box next to the movie description.

| action | horror | documentary | science fiction |

1. _____ A group of friends go to an old house in the woods for the weekend. What they don't know is that they are being watched by a scary monster.

2. _____ A police officer tries to stop a group of powerful criminals from stealing billions of dollars from a bank. Get ready for the best car chase you will see this year.

3. _____ In 2080, scientists travel to a remote planet to try to find life. What they find are intelligent aliens that look just like them, but who have their own plans for other planets.

4. _____ This movie is about Paris in the 1920s. The filmmakers use old photographs and jazz music to tell true stories about this special time in history.

C Complete the charts.

A movie I liked	Type of movie	Actors

A movie I didn't like	Type of movie	Actors

CONVERSATION

A Unscramble the words to make sentences. Add additional punctuation where necessary.

1. repeat / you / that? / can

2. catch / sorry / didn't / I / that

3. earlier / text / I / you / to / tried

4. there / I'll / at / see / eight / you

5. I / you / hear / again? / you / can / sorry / didn't / say / that

B Complete the conversation with the sentences in the box.

| Can you repeat that? I didn't hear you. | Got it. I'll see you there at seven-thirty. | I'm in a cafe. It's very busy. |
| Good. Where are you? It's so loud there! | Hey, Jacob. It's Mia. | |

Jacob: Hello?

Mia: _____

Jacob: How's it going?

Mia: _____

Jacob: _____

Mia: I see. Anyway, change of plans for tonight. We're going to go to the Moroccan restaurant, not the Spanish one. We are meeting at seven-thirty.

Jacob: _____

Mia: Sure. I said we're going to the Moroccan restaurant tonight, not the Spanish place. Can you meet us at seven-thirty?

Jacob: _____

Mia: OK. See you later.

Jacob: Bye.

C Now write a new conversation in your notebook. You have two tickets to a movie. Decide what type of movie you're going to see and at what time. Call your friend.

What's Playing? | **69**

GRAMMAR

A Complete the sentences with the present continuous.

My parents (1.) _____ (travel) to Cannes, France, for its international film festival next month! They (2.) _____ (go) because my mother (3.) _____ (receive) an award. She composes music for movies, and she (4.) _____ (be) honored for her work. They (5.) _____ (leave) for France on May 10th. My mom (6.) _____ (stay) for two weeks, but my father can only stay for ten days. They (7.) _____ (see) a few movies each day, and they (8.) _____ (meet) some movie stars, too!

B Write questions and answers about weekend plans. Use the present continuous.

	Javier	**Maki**	**Matt and Angie**
Saturday	go to the beach	clean her apartment	go shopping
Sunday	see a movie with his brother	study for a science exam	cook a big dinner

Javier

What's Javier doing on Saturday? 1. *He's going to the beach.* _____

2. _____ on Sunday? 3. _____

Maki

4. _____ 5. _____

6. _____ 7. _____

Matt and Angie

8. _____ 9. _____

10. _____ 11. _____

C Answer the questions about your own future plans.

1. What are you doing tonight?

   _____

2. What are you doing this weekend?

   _____

3. What are you doing next week?

   _____

B MOVIE REVIEWS

VOCABULARY AND GRAMMAR

A Match the adjectives with the opinions about movies.

1. boring
2. entertaining
3. funny
4. original
5. scary
6. surprising
7. violent

a. "I didn't expect that to happen."
b. "I loved it. It was so exciting!"
c. "I was so afraid, I had to close my eyes!"
d. "There was too much fighting in my opinion."
e. "I wasn't interested in the story. I fell asleep halfway through."
f. "It was so different. I've never seen a movie like it!"
g. "I couldn't stop laughing!"

B Complete the sentences with words from **A**. One word is not used.

It's Friday night, and you want to watch a movie. The question is, which one? You want to watch something **(1.)** _____ that will keep you interested. **(2.)** _____, long dramas always make you fall asleep. You could watch a **(3.)** _____ horror movie, like *The Ring*. It's very **(4.)** _____, so you never know what is going to happen next. But it's also a little **(5.)** _____. There's a lot of blood. It may not be the best to watch alone. How about a romantic comedy, like *Crazy Rich Asians*? It has a lot of romance, and there are some very **(6.)** _____ characters who will make you laugh.

C Complete the sentences with the correct adjective forms of the words in the box.

| bore | confuse | depress | excite | interest | surprise |

1. That movie was too _____. I couldn't understand the story.
2. I do the same thing every day at work. My job is really _____.
3. I was _____ when I heard the news. I really didn't expect it.
4. Are you _____ in classic movies?
5. I thought the movie was so sad. The story was really _____.
6. Action movies are very _____. They make me want to jump out of my seat.

D Write sentences with both the *-ing* and *-ed* forms of the words below. Use your own ideas.

1. boring _____
   bored _____
2. confusing _____
   confused _____
3. interesting _____
   Interested _____

Movie Reviews | 71

READING AND WRITING

A Read the movie listings.

In Theaters This Week

The Darkest Night In this new science fiction film, Brandon Carter stars as an astronaut who has a terrible accident. He is trapped on the dark side of the moon, with just a little food, air, and water. Can he survive? It's an exciting two hours!

Winter and Spring This movie is about two medical students who fall in love. They have big plans for the future: to get married, have a baby, and start a hospital for poor children. Then Paul (played by Matt Keene) gets very sick, and Melissa (Jessica Mays) must make a difficult decision.

My New Job You won't believe the plot of this new comedy, but it's very, very funny. A famous soccer star named Adriano (played by Paulo Costa) gets a job teaching kindergarten. The children do many crazy things, but Adriano learns some very important lessons from a little girl (played by Kaitlyn White). This is a great movie for families.

Don't Look in the Attic Rodney Jones and Shontelle Deane star in this scary movie. John and Susan are a young husband and wife who buy a new house. But their beautiful house has a terrible secret. How can they end their nightmare? Don't see this movie alone!

B Write the name of each movie from **A** under the correct picture.

1. _____

3. _____

2. _____

4. _____

C Write the words from the article.

1. _____ Paragraph 1: (noun) a person who travels to space
2. _____ Paragraph 1: (adjective) not able to escape or leave a place
3. _____ Paragraph 2: (adjective) relating to the practice of medicine
4. _____ Paragraph 2: (noun) choice about what to do
5. _____ Paragraph 3: (noun) story
6. _____ Paragraph 3: (noun) school for young children
7. _____ Paragraph 4: (adjective) awful
8. _____ Paragraph 4: (noun) bad dream

D Read the movie review. Then rewrite it, adding periods, commas, and capital letters.

> I saw *elizabeth's trip* last week it's a really exciting movie and there are some great actors in the cast the movie is about an old woman in new york named elizabeth she wants to visit her grandchildren in los angeles but she's afraid of airplanes she buys a bus ticket and starts an amazing trip she meets a lot of interesting and crazy characters on the bus she also sees some unusual places in the united states i really liked this movie a lot

E Write a review of a new movie. Use vocabulary from this unit.